Speaking con su Sombra

Speaking con su Sombra

Adrian Ernesto Cepeda

Copyright © 2021 by Adrian Cepeda
All rights reserved. no part of this publication may be reproduced,
distributed ut the prior written permission of the publisher, except in
the case of brief quotations embodied in critical reviews and certain
other noncommercial uses permitted by copyright law. For permission
requests, write to the publisher, addressed "attention: Permissions
Coordinator," at the e-mail address below.
davina@alegriamagazine.com

Library of Congress Control number: 2021919379

ISBN: 978-1-7379927-0-7

Published by Alegria Publishing
Book cover and layout by Carlos Mendoza

"A Mother and Child reunion, is so many [verses] away"

- Paul Simon

*"How powerfully I carry her within me.
My grief is tremendous, but my love is bigger."*

- Cheryl Strayed

Advance Praise for
Speaking con su Sombra

"In this maravilloso libro, Speaking con su Sombra, Ernesto Cepeda has brought his Mami to vivid vida on the page. In la poema, 'Mami Rose into the Sky,' he writes, "Rosa scent, eterno glow... always blessing our life." In la poema, 'Las Ultimas Palabras,' "Mami, gracias por la poesia...when I recite these stanzas/feeling renacido alive/in my mouth, mi boca/she speaks with me, glowing/luz on my face." I love that Ernesto has brought his Mami tongue Spanish into his poesia- it rings so true, de el corazøn, his roots la familia. Estas poemas create a vivid portrait of his relationship with his Mami- we never see her face, yet we see her face, hear her voice, clearly. A line that stays with me, "I never want our conversation to end," and I know it will never end. My conversation with my Mamacita continues after 65 years, especially las poemas-people have thanked me for her presence. A beautiful Mexican song- "Niña, si mi cantas, yo nunca muero...Child, if you sing me, I will never die." Ernesto's Mami will never die...their conversation, their poesia will never end. When you read este libro, you will remember your lost loved ones, and begin to sing together. La luz, la milagro. Siempre."

Alma Luz Villanueva, author de poesia, 'Gracias.'

"In this collection of poems, Speaking con su Sombra, by Ernesto Cepeda the reader will find some of the loftiest and most endearing lyrics to a mother so loved and cherished it brings a radiance of light to the reader's heart."

Jimmy Santiago Baca, author of *Singing at the Gates, When I Walk Through That Door, I Am* **and** *American Orphan*

"Speaking con su Sombra blooms with love like a rose and glitters with tears. A deeply felt tribute. A natural bilingual approach adds such depth and beauty."

Francesca Lia Block, author of *The Thorn Necklace: Healing Through Writing and the Creative process, Love Magik and the Weetzie Bat/ Dangerous Angels series.*

"The day Adrian Ernesto Cepeda's mother died, the sky had been overcast, but when she passed away, the sun broke through the clouds, golden and brilliant. Speaking con su Sombra holds a similar balance—these poems are steeped in grief and loss and sombre, but they also teem with love, with gratitude, with golden, brilliant, luz. A sense of playfulness is also threaded through this tender, aching collection—son becomes sun, becomes sonrisa, listen becomes glisten, words gleaming with their own light as well as the lingering light of Cepeda's mother and her influence on him and his poesía. A beautiful, moving, tribute."

Gayle Brandeis, author of *The Art of Misdiagnosis and Many Restless Concerns: The Victims of Countess Bathory Speak in Chorus*

"Adrian Ernesto Cepeda's Speaking con su Sombra is a poetry collection on healing from grief. Cepeda's story, told in English and Spanish, speaks to myriad people facing the loss of family and loved ones during a global pandemic. Early on, the author's mother asks him why he chose to live so far away from Tejas. During the course of these Sombra poems, we witness a son learning to be close to her across a far greater distance between the living and the ancestors. Cepeda accompanies readers through the mourning process, and finds healing by harvesting memories, and becoming grateful for the outcomes of his mother's loving kindness. Because of her, he is a poet. "I realize from my mourning," Cepeda writes, "mi Mami is no longer alive." But, by facing his emotions, and coming to terms with loss, he learns to "keep reopening the gift of today.""

Amy Shimshon-Santo, author of *Endless Bowls of Sky and Even the Milky Way is Undocumented.*

Mami Rose into the Sky	21
Una Última Vez	22
Tuesday's Have a Feel	23
I Am Trying to Answer Her	24
We Wrote the Saddest Poem Together	25
¿Dónde pongo mi tristeza?	26
I Still Can't Say Those Words	28
Happiness Used to Be a Friend of Mine	29
I Wouldn't Want to Take a Pill	30
Mi Mami's Nurse Lucilla Practices Tonglen	31
Tú	32
Mami	33
If Not for You	34
She is the Ghost	36
Every Day I Touch Her Crystal	37
El Catorce de Junio	38
The Story of my Life	39
Sometimes grief tastes like Azúcar	40
Papi says, I Could Lose 15-20 lbs.	42

Speaking con su Sombra

43	Julie had Julia
44	How I Miss Comiendo your Peanut Butter & Jelly Sandwich
46	Stirring Cocinas
47	I Never Dreamed of Heaven
48	Familia Tradition [No Rush]
50	I Miss You the Way Someone Drowning Remembers the Air
52	My Mami Called my Sueño
53	This House... Sans Her Spirit
54	I Still Hear Her
55	¿Cuántos años has estado Casado?
56	I Never Understood the Champagne Glasses
57	Por qué, Why Do You Live, Tan Lejos
58	Thirst Store Mysteries
60	Off to the Races
62	¿Te Diste Cuenta?
63	Shortcuts
64	Mi Mami Hated When my Hair Grew Long
66	Dear Mami [Letter]
72	I Wasn't Always the Devoted Son

Mami, I'm Not Ready to See You, Casi, Not Yet	74
Dónde Estás	75
Feeling So Useless	76
Will I Ever Be?	78
You are so Right, Kate	80
Here Come the Waves	81
Mi Mami Always Haunting my Fear	82
All I Feel is Miedo Fear	83
Sin Ti	84
Why Do I Keep Picturing...?	86
Las Últimas Palabras	87
Like a Camera Shuttering	88
All She Said	90
Sabes Lo Que Pienso	91
Detrás de la Ventana Mirando Afuera	92
¿Qué Recuerdo, y me Hace Más Falta?	93
Mi Mami Talks to her Plantas	94
Past Medianoche	95
La Nochebuena: Mil Novecientos Ochenta y Cinco	96

Speaking con su Sombra

98	What do I remember?
99	Everything I Write
100	The Son Who Brings You Sonrisas
101	As I Stand by Her Mar
102	What Does She See?
104	I Always Remember Dialing
106	Poesia Incompleto
107	El Milagro of Light
109	Nunca te Dije
110	¿A Dónde Vas?
112	Orlando to Key West [FLA road trip circa 1980]
114	I Saw You in Mis Sueños Last Night
116	¿Cuándo Dejaste de Hablar con Dios?
118	The Movie House is Our Church
120	En este Oscuro día de Noviembre 2017
122	Driving Us Back to the Hospital [in Joe's Car]
125	Afterword
129	Gracias y Agradecido
131	Aknowledgments

Forward:
Mi Mami gave me the gift of la poesía

When I was struggling to find my way, she encouraged me to write. I would not be a poet if it wasn't for mi Mami. Because of her, I can proudly say that I made it to graduate school and received my MFA and Post MFA. This is something she was most proud of. I've had over 200 poems published since 2013. None of this could ever have happened without mi Mami's encouragement.

I speak to her sombra daily. I hope that these poems will help those who have lost their own mothers. I urge you to keep the conversations going; I write every day, all the time. One of the first poems in this collection was inspired by the last moments she shared with me on this earth. When I am struggling with something, writing holds the answers. My way to communicate with mi Mami is through verse, and these poems represent the dialogues and the introspective rhymes that have kept me afloat through one of the most challenging times in my life. Although I speak in poems, it's important to keep the dialogue with the ones who have left us, to remind us, that pieces of them remain glowing while surrounding us.

Adrian Ernesto Cepeda

The poet Richard Siken once wrote, "If the dead are watching, I want them to see us writing, dancing, singing, painting. I want them to see that we still reach out to each other." Siken reflects what I've been experiencing. I feel my Mami as her shadow guides me every day at my writing desk. Even when I don't write poems about her, I feel like I am still speaking to her. I never want our conversations to end. Most days, when my fingers grace the keyboard, I feel like her shadow is illuminando my way through each poem. I never want to lose sight of the shadow. Sometimes I feel if I put my ear to each page of these poems, I can feel her speaking to me.

Some may ask, why craft this collection as bilingual poems? Before answering I am reminded of something Ingrid Rojas Contreras said in her piece "Translation as an Arithmetic of Loss " in The Paris Review" as she wrote, "Why didn't you write the novel in Spanish? This is a question I get all the time. Language is one of the things you sacrifice when you migrate. I wanted to be true to the toll of that sacrifice by making visible what exactly was being lost." In my case, I always spoke to mi Mami in English, and she always answered me in Spanish. As I got older, our conversations became more bilingual. So, this is the way I chose to honor her, in la amalgama of our native lenguas, reflecting in the ways I am still speaking to her in each poem.

Some will resonate with these lines by Natasha Trethewey: "Waking [...] with memory: my mother's last words/ spoken— after her death—in a dream: Do you know what it means/ to have a wound that never heals?" I know many of you have lost esposas, esposos, novias, novios, tias, tios, abuelas, abuelitos, Mami's y Papis. They say the personal is universal. With all the family members that have passed away in this horrible era of COVID, my wish is that by reading these poems, it will make you feel less alone with your grief. John Green once said, ""Grief does not change you. It reveals you."

Speaking con su Sombra

Poetry reveals all we are experiencing inside. La Poesia can be healing, and this is what we all need right now. I invite you to put your ear to the page and follow my journey honoring by her life, her passing and the gift of her legacy. As I remember the memoria of mi Mami, I am hoping these poemas can also honor yours, the ones you have lost in su familia.

Mami Rose into the Sky

Golden clouds opened up
witnessing as she already
brillante glowing her
way embracing sunlight.
We could feel her ascending
up into the cielo sky, all
that remains her gospel
spirit, her Rosa scent always
blessing our life, as Mami
and a wife, her presence,
her voz always a gift, now
resounding bright, she will
siempre shine in me… I'll never
forget before mis ojo eyes,
within this sight, from her
hospital sheets, our llorando
tears they already knew, when
we saw her eterno glow—
as our Mami Rose into
eternal light.

Adrian Ernesto Cepeda

Una Última vez

If I could hear
Mi Mami speak
Just one more time,
una última vez, I must
confess, I don't think
I would say single palabra
word. I just wouldn't want
waste a single second
and treasure every single
motherly sound, when she
exhales before her colloquial
wisdom, when she says mañana
es otro dia. no more interrupting
I would glisten this time,
not trying to make any
excuses instead I would
not get lost when she would
translate, instead
I would love to feel
the beaming revelations
grinning from mi Mami's
blooming Rosa face
that would loudly lecture
me if I close mis ojos
and truly concentrate
I can hear her guidance.
How I miss her cielo voice
raising in the clouds, so clear
volume her louder, fading
now no se viase, her
voice inside me, still
speaking fuerte near
and strong.

Tuesday's Have a Feel

Although so many preguntas
questions linger, ringing
over and over, flashing
mi Mami's sweet caramello
face over and over en mi
mente mind... I continue
picture her speaker voz
and keep redialing razones
over and over so many reasons,
no matter how many times
I ask recalling Tuesday,
on el teléfono, our talks
are now filled with too much
silencio. No matter how many
times I keep dialing up her
last memory face, all I hear
is dial tones wishing, she
was still there at her casa
home– Martes are the worst
as this silence always reminds,
no quiero creer, I don't want
to believe this cold empty
touchtone feeling. Me siento
solo as I sit alone, when I clutch
my loudest phone resounding
so many recuerdos, remembering
how I miss mi Mami and her
morning sonrisa laughter. Even
though it's still too quiet,
I never want to hang up...
as the endless ringing
from within my head,
keeps asking– ¿por qué?
Why is she gone? I fear–
there'll never be an answer

*"The World wants to know
what I am made of. I am trying
to find a way
to answer Her."*

- Robin Coste Lewis

I Am Trying to Answer Her

With every line, I reignite
my voice, these wide rule
lines are my only stage,
this pen is my microphone
watch me grip as ink gushes
out loudly within stanza
creation a present, gifted
me by mi Mami, I know
she is watching me, ashes
blues crystalized, above
as I write this, click closer
to the last line, I always
press save, I can feel her
glowing, adelante hijo.
keep finding your voice,
with every verse, each rhyme
I hear you answer.

We Wrote the Saddest Poem Together

That Saturday, at low noon, united
as a family, all the Amor gathering
between us, experiencing the light,
the sky above, the rays, coming from
the blinds into the room, watching
our Mother soaring away from us, her
final breath, from the hospital bed,
gasping all the love from our tearing
sights, watching with eyes filling
tears for the last time seeing
my Papi clutching the love
from our Mami, his wife, lifting
up from this hospital bed,
fading from our presence,
watching her disappear, gifting
all of us with the final glow–
as we write this poem arms
bracing together, so thankful
we could see the last line, her cafe
eyes fading inside her final sunset.

It's then I ask you, mama, my mother,
my heart, my mother, my heart, my mother,
mama, the sadness I feel. Where do I put it?

Where, mama?

- Elena Poniatowska, from *"La Flor de Lis,"*

published c. January 2011
¿Dónde pongo mi tristeza?

Where do I put all
my sadness, Mami?
You used to soothingly
say, telling me to cálmese–
and I would exhale
my attack de pánico would
slowly subside but now
that you've dissolved into
the most holy and beautiful
of spirits, where can
my anxiety go? There's
no one left to tell me where
to place all the fear, you
left me to face la tormenta
while drowning adentro
inside all this miedo that comes
like waves olas de hurricane.
No stopping these second
thought winds, forecasting
my next inner storm, I miss
reaching out teléfono dial
you and your voice would
calm la tempestad hurling

Speaking con su Sombra

within, now I imagine
your calming laugher like
overcast sunshine above
wanting to appear brillante
while I stand in darkness
sombra overshadowing me
I remember all you told me
and sometimes I listen
to your most soulful voz
speaking to me en mi mente,
I need to find a place to put
all this tension, I just
miss the goddess rays
when your voice would
arrive and I could flow
inside and absorb
the turbulent downpours
mis ojos tears loves to flood
way past the days you would
quiet the rain, though mis ojos
still wet, peaking from inside
Pasolini was right, it's not
That the dead do not speak,
it's that we forgot how to hear
them. With eyes open, now
I listen close and I feel her
sol like su voz, no longer
overcast, lo oigo glowing
clearly speaking distante near.

Adrian Ernesto Cepeda

I Still Can't Say Those Words

Every morning when I awaken
she's always disappearing, no
different, somehow today
is worse. On this holiday
of Mother's does anybody
ever thinks about the loneliest
ones like me, orphaned feeling–
thank you, Hallmark, 1-800
Flowers, every heart shaped
candy shop, I am lost in sees
of chocolate reminders, when
the alarm rings waking up
on this Sunday, mouthing
this half-empty refrain, the exile,
I am, myself, the shadow–
too many letters scarlet reframed
now they whisper out of my ear
sight what they can never tell me,
I have not asked to be reborn,
redefined. all that remains–
this boy has unfortunately become
renamed the two-word reminding
me, once I was, no longer a son–
un hijo sin Madre, any tongue
will translate, because she no
longer rings me, I am the one
they call–motherless child.

Happiness Used to Be a Friend of Mine

I've been asked, happy,
are you ever? I used
to know what that word
meant…feeling moments
of joy my cheeks basking
in blushing grins blowing
out cumpleaños candles
but since she's passed
I am content in the gift
of the present, watching
LA's Galaxy Zlatan score
that golazo from midfield
and then after the final
whistle remembering
I watched mi Mami's soul
flow back into el sol, recalling
how hungry I was and even
though it's been nine
months I am still mourning
while some days are harder
to swallow that others,
realizing happiness used
to be a friend of mine
and despite what my therapist
claims, no pill is never
going to fix me ever.

I Wouldn't Want to Take a Pill

Inhale a hit, drown myself
in shots, the gift is embracing
all of this, the loss, the sobbed
shaped hole that throbs deep
inside like a wound, always
pulsating painful mental souvenirs
that keep me showering even
more tears, although some nights,
awake, I feel so drained, all
that I know, despite all the grief
that I behold, the visions flashing
mi Mami's last comatose breath
I face while grieving, and although
I may cry out like la llorna,
remembering I can see now
the dead can dance toward
the within, inside our most agonizing
refrains, leaving us spinning, confused
rhythms, on why she had to fade
away as the sound of her passing
always amplifies…I long to keep
reexperiencing all these memories
that will eternally scar me like
often reveal inner tattoo wounds
agony seldomly never heals.

Mi Mami's Nurse Lucilla Practices Tonglen

More than just
a nursing procedure–
this meditation she practices
in her scrubs, we watch
palms ready, by moistening
mi Mami's dry sky and
lubricating softly by taking
in my mother's agony into
her own heart. So selfless
as Lucilla's calm face shows
no anguish as she internalizes
mi Mami's pain. I love the way
she sweetly talks, softly almost
whispering long blushing
salon like conversations as if
she and mi Mami is awake
and they are lifelong vida
amigas, but these one-way talks
help my mother, I can tell as her
eyes light up from Lucilla's healing
touch, more than feel, not religion,
more softening connection,
this practice of Tonglen
not just for kneading skin,
from each healing massage
therapy of aroma, fingers
greeting mi Mami's acupressure
body points, slowly touching
heartbeats, although they might
have been strangers out of this ICU
hospital room, despite the lengua
differences Lucilla, she speaks
with her magically wrinkled
nursing hands, her fingertips
always loves to listen.

Tú

Shadowing behind, always
pendiente, radiating
siempre creyendo en mí,
proud of my crescendo
glowing creciendo
your belief grows, rising
even from esta distancia
you were the cielo
to my skies, reflejando
the vinyl disco I spun
your favorite canción
preferida, remembering
always the days we sung
juntos in harmony–
no matter how many
miles lejos, you,
shadowing behind always
pendiente, following
su hijo continuado
a soñar, cantando
mis poemas, el sol
of your son.

Mami

Even though
you've desaparecido
your distant presence
I can still feel. Often, I try
te llamo, reaching out to call
you but as I summon
my voice, two years,
I realize it's been almost
dos años, you can never
reply, but I am hoping
one day you will answer
me, so many times I deslumbro
glare into your vidrio glass figurine
although you glow beautifully
in sunlight, most days your luz
del sol leaves me azul drowning
days even though I'm on land
in my mind swimming laps
ahogándome at my desk,
en mi escritorio, I no longer
can conceal my ocean blues.
I just want to feel your voz
talk back but there's nothing
but dead air, static lines,
this is why I keep redialing
rhymes, nothing I could say
aloud, want to hear you
for a segundo this is why
I quiet mi boca con prudencia–
Still mesmerized by your words
in memoriam, I still long
to listen to you.

If Not for You

All the way, Mami,
hearing me refrain
But it takes so long
still you always turned
up el radio, driving me
to la pulga, Flea Market
for my belated Navidad
gift, near the back we
followed the footsteps
of guitars, looking up
on the wall of expensive
vinyl you told el hombre
with the long curly gray
barba, knowing I wanted All
Things Must Pass, triple

Speaking con su Sombra

LP still wrapped up,
el disco used, on the way
back home you told me
when I was in your barriga
el radio en la cuidad de
Nueva York always played
"My Sweet Lord," the palabras
you loved I really want
to see you, singing to me,
were the first words you
learned in ingles. Every time
I drop the record needle on
the groove takes me back
you driving me as I held
my triple vinyl records
hearing George's riffs as we
both played la air guitarra
with our dedo fingers. Even
now that you are up there, farther
way, I really want to show
you, Mami, I still love singing
cantando, here's hoping
when I'm driving in my car
windows roll down, turning
up our song, looking
at the cielo skies, between
la Hallelujah chorus, our sweet
Dios can feel me serenading you.

She is the Ghost

Silently breathing
beside me, always
feeling her voice–
I long to reply but she's
like her call, mi Mami
rarely replies, she is
beyond answers–
I hear her in memories
flashes bringing me back
to Yesterday, although
I feel like melting
snowballs, I hate
to grip as my little
niño pequeño hands
she once could warm,
why do I feel like I am
shivering outside waiting
to awaken teeth ratting
rising every day discontented
winter forecast, although
the sun still rises, I realize
from my mourning, mi Mami
is no longer alive.

Every Day I Touch Her Crystal

As she glows above me,
somehow, it still doesn't
feel like three hundred
and sixty-five days, un
año calendario and she
is still gone but I feel her
closer to me like an invisible
presencia when I reopen
mis ojos, with my eyes,
I envision her appearing
in between lines when
I press down on the keys,
making music with palabras
my voice singing reconnecting
with her alma sparks
inside me, with my words,
her advice I keep unwrapping,
volumes so sweet and clearly
as she glows brillante within me,
every day touching her crystal
I can hear her whisper sigue
abrazando el regalo–
within each cry I feel her
reflect and magnify
that I keep reopening
the gift of today.

El Catorce de Junio
[en el año mil novecientos setenta y uno]

Outside está nevando, inside
I'm channeling static tiredness
it's snowing beauty, reflecting
in my arms, mi cuerpo tired
cansado, but I am still
muy emociando con mi
hijo, my son is also rising
maybe I'll name him Ernesto
after my favorite escritor,
Hemingway hoping he loves
to put his pensamientos to pen;
I can feel him rustling despierto,
amen already awakened
to my Americano hijo already
rustling in my hospital room,
knowing one day, he may fight
me, gritando at times, I try
calming his llorando spirit
by perhaps sharing this
cuento will do: "las
banderas are flying, on
Flag Day, mi hijo, only
for you." And I'll continue
glowing brioso & proud
from this instance and maybe
by listening and creating Neruda
versos con juicio, my little mentira
might actually ring true.

The Story of my Life

My eyes arrived restless–
kicking with blindness
ascending,
even when reached
astray you were always
there defending me,
inside, as I crawled
to you, your embrace
always ready to face me
and my clever honesty
of my carless cracked
lines. I walk with you
in mis sueños y mi corazón
beating proudest before
reaching out to fly…
I soar through heights
a relative unknown–
realizing this, I rarely
float alone, su voz
my guide, like a wink
in all your truths, the reasons
why, the story of my life
would simply be meaningless
without you-siempre
by my side.

Adrian Ernesto Cepeda

Sometimes grief tastes like Azúcar

Reminding me of el arroz
con leche you would simmer
on the stove, some days
even in my Angeles apartamento
un millón de millas from our
casa on Burlington Ave. donde
estarías standing al frente de
la estufa, like una conductora,
la cuchara your baton as you
stirred adding so many scrumptious
flavors, milk condensed from
the can, sticks of canela cinnamon
crescendos of aromas mouth
sumamente watering apetitoso
wanting to taste the symphonic
harmonies percolating inside
la cacerola, I remember standing
in front of this saucepan waiting
for you to hand me the spoon for
el primer sabor, and savoring
the melodic overtures inside
mi boca, you should have
taken a bow, standing ovación
de pie, we were the lucky ones
to have tasted the philharmonic

Speaking con su Sombra

Delicia, every noche.
And some nights, in my own cocina,
pienso all your recetas that will never
be treasured, cada uno of your
dishes, live in mi memoria of
standing in la cocina, the aroma
of grief has a flavor I want
to swallow but the aftertaste
remains a sugary suite sonata
that lingers inside after all
these años of tears, I remain
unquenchable in loss.

Thank You Hieu Minh Nguyen

Adrian Ernesto Cepeda

Papi says, I Could Lose 15-20 lbs

But the sadness, just like
my hambre never waits,
always hungering to find
me, within these extra
pounds, libras, never belly
full, mi barriga always
eating me, feeling empty
dressed muy apretado
in this too tight black suit,
some days during la comedia
I can still hear her la cocina
voz from the kitchen, telling
me to termina tu plato, so
in her honor, I always finish
my plate; mi Papi doesn't realize,
I just don't agonize over
almuerzo, even during
desayuno mourning, sorrow
simmers so many flavors
with each thankful bite, Mami's
muerte passing keeps devouring me.
instead of saying grace, I always
offer her my appetite.

Julie had Julia

…and being her niño child,
I had mi Mami stirring
back standing in front
of la estufa trying to remember
all those recetas, I recall inhaling
the steam like a cocinero's
dinner dream, when she
baked so many aromas
en la cocina the spices
bailando danced together
when added pimenta and salt
to the sartén, pots and pans
bubbling in symphony,
trying to conjure up
those same delicioso
recipes cantando…

Just like Julie could feel
and sentir, hearing Julia's
instructions, mi Mami
speaks to me, recuerda
to keep stirring as she
calls me El Chef, sharing
her especias directions,
reminding me to keep
cocinando con su corazón,
by roasting those flavors
your familia will adore
el sabor of every bite
and just like Mami
gleamed from Julia,
with any lengua,
todos soñamos, we
all long to inspire-
family toasting
while our aftertastes
delectably mouthing–
bon appetite.

Adrian Ernesto Cepeda

*How I Miss Comiendo
your Peanut Butter
& Jelly Sandwich*

No one could ever make it
like you, pan lightly toastado
and the way, Mami, you would
perfectly layer con el cuchillo
the exacta and la perfecta
amount of rojo raspberry
jelly and the extra creamy
Jiff, leaving it en la mesa
and even know I can still
taste the aroma of melted
mermelada with peanut butter
todavía llama a mis sentidos,
my tastebuds would always
try to recreate the prefect
PB&J but I would always
over-toast the bread or
spread too much Jiff
and some days the jelly
would overflow outside

the slices of burnt bread.
Now que tengo cincuenta
años de edad, I can no longer
comer my favorite sandwich,
the Jiff makes my stomach
volcano in acid reflux. Even
now, ¿Cómo podría olvidarlo?
The sensation of saborear
each one of your delicioso
dishes imagine el plato
waiting for me, mi boca
recuredas now that you
are lejos, gone, my memory
of you, mi sueño inspires–
el sabor that still calls me,
my tastebuds wish I could
answer, to show you I still
remember, waking up still
savoring, I nunca will forget,
despite la fecha on the viejo
bread, la memoria flavor
of mi favorite almuerzo
contigo will never expire.

Stirring Cocinas

I watched you stirring
pots, spicing Papi's lengua,
with arroz con pollo, patacones
fritos, maíz del amor cada
noche you cured mi hambre.
Taught me, life's sabor. I listened
with azúcar tastes that would
flour me– sugar crème cheers
mi boca– drops hunger smile–
sonrisa, sweetness toast you,
con mi copa de gracias, Mami
Colombiana—Háblame
de postre delicioso, helado rico,
fresas ice cream a la mode.
All it takes is one whipped
spoonful, dulce de leche
swallowing reminders
aromas of Arequipe kitchens–
your apron string always stirs
my tastes of home.

I Never Dreamed of Heaven

Until we set you alight
in cremation colores
smoke de celeste like
ashes floating angelic
into the clouds. But
I keep replaying
your voz still percolating
in my ears like songs
that glimmer profound
lessons, I once tried to
bury inside. Why am I
afraid to weep, you
are not in my sleep,
it's a like a dream,
a sueño, I wish
to wake up sweating
in fear, I need to arise
in risilla giggles,
and embrace your
laughter, reign
your suicio on me
from the skies
let me color tan canela
and your presence will
have me mourning luto
lumber once again.

Adrian Ernesto Cepeda

Familia Tradition
[No Rush]

As time crawls,
snow bells keep jingling,
Papi's still snoring,
our PJ's keep itching impatience,
the chimney thirsting
no presents before OJ
el jugo de naranja–
as Mami calls it
too pulpy for my tongue;
Awaken to darkness and tree lights;
our sueños, so spoiled
this madness dreaming of new gifts
runs through all of us.
My little brother
Joe keeps peaking around
unwrapped corners
as the oldest Rene and his four eyes
has x-ray visions,
with his superpower
my older hermano
ready to sleigh icicle paper
at a single bound.
This leaves me, the one in the middle
the lookout for danger,
lurking, we've been
midnight creeping
under silver glowed X-mas branches–

Will Mami y Papi ever wake up?
Awaiting miracle of our mañana
when finally arriving like a symphony
stage conductor, relighting his greeting–
the opening of his door finally

my Father arises morning
of Buenos dias choruses:
to the sounds of Händel's Hallelujah
cielo bellowing, "¿Están listos?"

We're ready!
Surprises Mami's grin
unwrapping our excitement–
toasting even more shots of Orange Juice
Dad downs his with egg
on the bottom, watches with glee
with each gulp tries to gaggle his sons.
Laughter rises from Papi's Santa
Simpático unshaven sweater chest.
Flexing voiced muscles,
our waited argument fades,
blinks then framing my favorite…
besos, regalos: joyful, our presence
mi Mami's gusting thankful reminders–

she always remembers
how the melting of rivals
once frosty, brothers united
with our fireplace glasses
now raised without voices
angered in disgust.
Still thirsty, anticipating
tradition the sharing of gifts
can never be rushed.
As tears of familia
now so triumphantly hugs
as our presents are always
exchanged with abrazos of trust.

I Miss You the Way Someone Drowning Remembers the Air

>Looking at these lines
>vast and blank like an ocean
>wide, as I sit here gasping
>just like I saw you taking
>in those last breaths.

Speaking con su Sombra

There are no Birthday canadales
to blow out this year.
There are just more preguntas
you are not here to answer
me, my phone remains
silent and you are no longer
on the other end, just static
I wish you could ring me
and say "hijo" just one last
time, so you would listen
to me and embracing
mis palabras like you loved
to do, I miss your long distance
abrazos, now I am just swimming
my mind keeps wading
the deep waves keep coming
pulling me under
and despite all the splashing
I am still shivering
my mind adrift
trying to face that you
will never glisten
and this still leaves me
numb in mis oidos, ears
wanting to receive and
hear you again, instead
this page and now, as I try
to grip these palabras–
my ink keeps on dripping
llorando tears, all over.
Thank You Tim Seibles

Adrian Ernesto Cepeda

My Mami Called my Sueño

In my dream she left
a mensaje from the other
side, Hijo, she started
speaking, ella comenzó
a hablar in a very loud
jubilosa voice, Me gusta
los poemas, she said like
she was holding my new
book, embracing Flashes
and Verses from el cielo.
I remember rewinding and
listening over and over
to her sweetest cariñoso
static message. Like a poem
I wanted to dive inside her
palabras and swim within
los felicidades of all her words.
Still even when mi Mami
speaks from beyond, ella sueña–
she always sonriente sounds
like her voz of home.

This House... Sans Her Spirit
"I knew nothing but shadows and I thought them to be real."
– Oscar Wilde

        All the glasses you displayed
        now glow half empty thirsting
        for you like the walls hearing
        the tiles are now much to quiet
        so used to hear your midnight
        shuffling with chanclas, socks
        in slippers, opening cupboards
        that miss your touch, even
        the couches long for your light
        weight, still waiting to save
        you a seat. The carpet misses
        your footprints, the doors never
        want to reopen again, staying
        locked inside with all the memories
        and you hold the keys, this casa
        is haunted, your house is missing
        your presencia. When I listen
        to the painting you picked out
        for the la pared, they whisper
        exhibiting so little color in voices
        telling me we can hear the sink drips
        most nights, showers this palace
        with sadness, Mami we keep waiting
        for your reawakening, the plants
        miss the way you spoke life to root
        now wilting, do you miss your leaves?
        This stillness much to quiet
        without your spirit, even the foundation
        grass is drying tears, cactus cries
        longing for your quintessence
        this valiant estate actually perceives–
        su casa once glowed silently
        can you feel behind these gates
        your palacio privately grieve?

I Still Hear Her

My Mami is in this first line
la primera línea, here, she always
appears even when I don't expect
to feel her, she arrives in a thought
cloud, a daydream and a late night
pensamiento, I miss the sound
of her voice when she would
instantly, sin paradas, lift me
up just by saying "¡Hola, Poeta!"
Pero en este momento there is too
much silencio. So now, she lives,
breathes and dances within these
poemas, this gift she gave me,
I unwrap this presente, never
want to stop our stanza conversación
even when I reach el fin using these
keys with one touch, she unlocks so much–
I hear my Mami's voz answer me inside
these last line verses, she will always
resonar… write through me.

¿Cuántos años has estado Casado?

My mother enquires,
asking how these seven
years have been to her once
eternally spoiled bachelor,
mi Mami once raised.
Without pausing, I reply,
"El matrimonio es anything
but fácil. But, making
the leap has been the most
fulfilling jump I have
ever versed." And
best of all, in between

the silence all that still
ignites from mi corazón–
I never tell her how, once
testy, the arousing poems
keep coming, as our naked
rhymes arrive, excited
with each arising so much
harder down… as her esposo,
I love it when nakedly
enrapturing… she whispers
want to bellow? I respond

just like my first vows–
mi Amor, of course, I do.

I Never Understood the Champagne Glasses

When I was younger in my tennis
racket pajamas watching
the countdown at midnight,
as the ball dropped
when it turned 12:01 AM,
despite the abrazo hugs
and beso kisses, I never
felt any different, what
has changed from a minute
ago? I do remember instead
of toasting glasses, wine
or beer, you taught me to eat
one grape for every month
of the happy new year. Telling
me it was for buena luck. The room
would laugh as I would always eat
them too fast, now when I swallow
this tradition, it's not the same,
with every grape is an aftertaste
without you, this año nuevo
rings will never have the same
refrain.

Por Qué, Why Do You Live, *Tan Lejos*

I needed my distance, as I told
my Pali cohort sister Natalie
understanding why I lived
so far away from mi familia
in San Antonio, instead
more than space, I needed
to feel these states to remind
although this distance reflected
a longing, with each mile between
us revealed a closeness, a love
that greeted the baggage of all
the words I left unsaid. Although
I missed mi Mami, my father
and mis hermanos, some nights
I need to leave them relatively
unpacked, rekindling every descendant
redefinition I sought and continues
to speak, beseeching everyone
I love to embrace inside my head.

Adrian Ernesto Cepeda

Thrift Store Mysteries

I can still hear her, mi Mami
porque, why would you want
to know someone else's ropa–
clothes? Cochino, is what she
would tell me over and over
and of course being the grosero
treinta-something boy/man-child
that I was I had to go just to see
the blushing annoyance on her
rosy roja caramella tan cara
cheeks. What mi Mami never
wanted to entender were los
cuentos, the stories, so many
untold inside the aisles of Good
Will. So many inanimate voices,
ready to speak to me. What
happened to the wilted now
faded off white matrimonio
boda dress. Holding up, I picture
aromas of a mal conceived
medianoche Vegas wedding–
a once beaming siren now
dimming in regrets, wanting
to forget the night, she would
replay in her mind, just like
the hombre who once sported

the azul prom tuxedo suit,
almost pristine with a hint
of Southern Comfort, stains
of a chaser memories of Old
Style cerveza tell me this
chico never found his lucky
señorita, or else he would
have kept and treasured his

suerte Buena threads, that
ooze smooth cool like
a Fonzi leather chaqueta
de cuero, even Mami would
be impresionada with this
one. How many motorcycle
rides did this masterpiece
of fabric experience before
the wife made the owner
donate— just by the aroma
you could tell she didn't want
all the lonely neighborhood
esposas y lobas divorciadas
sniffing around her once malo
bad boy, now tamed sin
his immortal threads like
superman domesticated
without his cape. All of these
cuentos on every rack, hanging
ready for further adventures—
reminding me when I would
arrive home, before logging into
AOL, ready to hear mi favorito
90s phrase, you've got mail.
I can hear mi Mami ordering
Me to wash and lavate sus
sucias manos— she not knowing
in my closet I scored a vintage
blanca y negra camisa, perfecto
para Mardi Gras, she may never
enterder, giving new life, to
a shirt like this, yearning
to experience new skin, placing
mi oreja to the fabric and feel
their anticipación of so many
stories these colores, pockets
and collars ready to behold

Off to the Races

I was the one always replaying
that same broken record song,
the one you hated with all
the scratches, the feedback
turned up all my mistakes,
Apaga las Rosas, you would grita
yell at me to turn off my G'n'R,
Patience, you had no for my self
destructive appetite. You oyendo
hearing me run, from my bedroom, across
the hallway to the bathroom so many
times, still drunk even as you stood
over me, as I heard Papi burlarse mock,
shouting, he's off to the races again
and you, no sympathy for your li'l diablo,
telling me how I shouldn't be a borracho,
were you celosa jealous as I embraced
the porcelain goddess, instead of you,
believing she understood, my heaves,
everything I left there left me empty,
flushing away my inner demons you
tried keeping down, always regurgitated
up, uncaged me grounded for so many
years, cause you many more midnights
waiting for me to stumble home, you
always feared the worst in me
and I never disappointed–me
as a teenager and twenty something

Speaking con su Sombra

boychild, ¿Cómo aguantaste? How
did you put up with the spoiled niño
inside? You realize Mami, I had to leave,
to take my own trips, inhale so many more
hits, even more shots, you could never
protect me from swerving down mi camino
de exceso, this road of excess lead me to this
palacio of wisdom, did you ever think I would
make it? Seeing me there on la carpeta, pale,
stomach growling in agony, dizzy mareado
to the world, yes part of me wanted to drown
myself in every botella of rum, who needed
a beer when I was my own chaser. Trying
to outrun my own misstep, tripping over
who I loathed the most, the one who always
tripped over his own words. I hated the sound
of my own voice, and worse how I looked
so flaquito bony in the mirror. I was a skeleton
trying to rush into my grave, but despite all,
you ignited me, never shut me out, listened
even as I was drifting lost ghost like
in the dark when I was an hombre invisible,
you encouraged me to pen mis palabras,
escribe uno para mí, you urging me
and finally, I caught my glimpse on the page,
with every key I pressed down reflected
the true me, far from brave, glaring
at the screen no longer heaving— instead
of trashing my words, every stanza creada
in that basement room in Pasadena, you
taught me not to erase the body of mis poemas.

Adrian Ernesto Cepeda

¿Te Diste Cuenta?

I once devoured the petals
of Ava's jardín, she enticingly
giving me a lesson privada,
on your bed, mi instructor
de poesía with her well-aged
lengua wisdom, a pluma
holding her hair up in a bun
con juicio and savoring her
sabor, she taught me nuevoas
palabras as Ava loved turning
out apaga las luces, and we
created our own poems in la
oscura dark, mouthing new
direcciones, sharing the más
excitante instrucciones, learning
on su cama as our nuestro coro
de voces recited cuerpo rimas
past medianoche. She said We can...
and directed me in all the spaces
ritmos and rhymes could be
reclaimed, as we swam
desnudo on su cama,
our cuerpo bodies read each
other from the spine to our back
softcovers. I know Mama, I could
already picture the worried
look of '¿did our vecino neighbors,
who you never talk to, overhear
all los desnudo odes we created?'
Who needs Playboy when I loved
mouthing all of Ava's stanzas
provocativos, no te diste cuenta
as she led instructing me her
most devoted pupil focusing
ojos, abierto labios savoring
each lesson on how to awaken
her most sensual poema.

Shortcuts

He turns left and right,
break, pedaling faster
trying to avoid the jamming
of traffic, and all those idling
in red stopped lights. But even
with every signal, seeking
the short cuts, he returns
to the same place, always
reflecting mi Mami's voice,
closer than she actually
reappears, in his rearview,
feeling exhaust when waiting
behind so my cars, she always
knew, there are no expressway
short cuts, continue mapping
your patience, better, stay
on the road; will he ever remember
her direction… advice? No matter
how long it takes, ignore every short
cut, always treasure the drive
of this freeway, horizon ahead–
and, you will always go far.

Adrian Ernesto Cepeda

Mi Mami Hated When my Hair Grew Long

I remember when she would
place newspaper in bathroom and
mis hermanos and I would line up
in our calzoncillos, waiting as she
would have us hold up the cover
of el disco record of Los Beatles
A Hard Day's Night. Although
I loved the way she used the same
tijeras that she would wrap
our reglaos de navidad, sometimes
when I listen to the title cut it brings
me back to the snip, snipping, sitting
on the toilet in el baño, watching
all our little pelos fall, Mami would
say, 'adiós pelitos largos" as we would
watch our brown hair flakes falling like
snow. Although I loved those Fab Four
haircuts. Yesterday, as I walked away
from the San Marino Barber shop,
glaring at my reflection, knowing
that mi Mami would love this haircut
I do wonder why she only wanted her
hijos to have short crew cuts? Did it
have to do with the secret novio

boyfriend she had in high school,
Mami would describe him as el único
in his leather chaqueta de cuero
that would pick her up from escuela
secundaria in his motocicleta. Did
she never forget the way his long
hair would smell as he would drive
her around those small curvy Bogotá
streets? Was she enamored with his
long curly rizado hair, flowing
in the breeze, so much exhaust
that she would rest her head on his
leather jacket, he would cruise
so fast that she clutched on never
wanting to let go. But one day she
did, el unico was not enough, Mami
wanted more than someone who would
honk with long hair shades like gafas
del sol, leather jacket motorbike mystery
man. Is this why she wanted her sons
with short haircuts? The long curls
reminded her of the one who rode
away, the scent of his pelo, simpre
oliendo su aroma, in the breeze,
maybe some days this rider easy
on her ojo eyes, would flashback
motorcycle hombre honking in
her memoria this time wishing
he would never leave?

Dear Mami,

Today is going to be a busy day. Not only am I going to the store, but I need to lavar mi ropa. I need to keep my routines up and going. Especially since reading Plath's biography it reminds me of how many years I was depressed and instances when I had thoughts of hurting myself, I am not proud of these thoughts, but back then when I was in my teens and twenties, I was a very sad joven/hombre. It's nothing that you and Papi did. You gave us so much love and security. Sadly, it's how I felt inside about myself. I had the hardest time making friends and it was even harder trying to meet and keep a novia. It took me years to find my own self-confidence. This is why I had to move away. I needed to find something inside of me to ignite a fire to give me self-assuredness and a spark to want to thrive and after moving to many different places and outlasting my depression, I found my calling and home in Los Angeles.

Speaking of destiny. I don't think we ever talked about this. Why I kept leaving home to live on my own. I was very unhappy with myself. I was weak, I was spoiled and one day I realized my destiny was never going to be in Texas. I needed to go explore and live alone. You know what the best part of leaving home and living in a place out of state, coming back home to visit you and la familia. You know that we always got along better from a distance. This is not a bad thing, it's just the truth. I was on a journey. This journey was internal and also continental as it led me to where I needed to be. Think about it, if I had not left Texas, I would not have lived in Chicago, met Laura, moved to California, and eventually met Michelle. I learned that it's these leaps of faith, even the stumbles, the falls, the heartbreaks, and the mistakes that led me to the place and the one

I was meant to be with. All the pain, doubt, missteps
were all worth it, as this journey made me the poet
and published author that I am today. Because of all
I experienced, good and bad, now, I appreciate it all.
Every day I wake up so thankful, I am here con mi
esposa, mi gatico and our li'l apartamento home is in
Los Angeles.

You know I always loved watching movies and films
set in the City of Angels, today when I saw Gentefied,
I cried during a scene. You know I have a framed
photograph of you, on the table next to my chair in the
living room. I need it there, so you are always with me. I
can turn to you and it feels like you are with me.

Last night, as we watched Gentefied, while looking at
your photograph feeling your presence next to me, I
cried because I wish you could be here to experience
my success. I need you to know, mis éxitos are
your successes; I realize now this is what struck me
emotionally and why I cried while watching this episode.
I needed to verbalize and let it out, to understand why
I was so sad for these past three years. I know you are
here with us but I just wanted you to be present so I can
embrace you and say Thank You, Mil Gracias, Mami!

Because of the recurring of my sadness, Michelle and
I talked about the time we were living in la casa en
Summit Creek and I was so depressed that for a moment
I pondered suicide. Then the phone rang, and el Aleman
called me, and I realized I am not alone, and I forgot
about it. You could say Karl saved my life there, just be
calling me, wanting to see how I was doing.

Years later when I lived in Chicago after Laura first left
me that was one of the worst times, I was so depressed.

I recall walking every morning, I was so unhappy. And then when I moved to California to be with her and we broke up, yet again. When I lived in the hatch, the basement room in Pasadena, I was in literal darkness. That was the time I saw a therapist and it helped. Even then I didn't want to believe I had depression. It had to take a pandemic and all the horrible symptoms I experienced to finally admit I was always suffering from anxiety and depression.

Reading Heather Clark's bio on Plath, has really made me ponder where my depression started. I believe that it may have had it's roots in Ann Arbor, being constantly teased for having a stutter. One kid actually made fun of me saying I probably stuttered while I went to the bathroom. Although, the outside environment may have contributed to mi depression, I don't want you to think I blame you or Papi, this is nobody's fault. We had some amazing times in Laredo. I love for all you have done for you us and what you still do for our familia now that you have transitioned. I am just thinking about this for me. No blame. No anger. Just wondering how long have I been suffering with depression? And why was I so afraid to admit it and tell you and Papi about how unhappy I was. This is all on me. Some days I wish I had the strength to admit to you and Papi all the pain I was experiencing inside so much sooner than now.

Speaking of sadness, we never talked about it but when I flew into San Antonio, the night before you died, seeing you on the bed was so traumatizing for me. Seeing you on the bed, you looked like someone had hurt you in the face. I was so upset. What I remember most was the next day, it was as if you were waiting for me to transition. I will never forget it. I was sitting across from you, Mami, watching you, Papi was on the phone and I could tell something was going to happen. I made Papi aware and we all stood there watching. And then the most amazing thing happened. That morning, was an overcast day in San Antonio, and when you died, as your soul transitioned over, the sun came out. It was the most beautiful thing. I read about how this same thing happened to George Harrison's family when he died. This is a rare thing. Looking back, I am so thankful I made it and flew in to be with you Mami. I needed to be there. And somehow, I knew, you felt, I was there. You did not want to transition and die without me there. Thank You for waiting for me.

There was one person, a nurse in the hospice wing of the hospital that was so kind, loving, sweet and nice to you. She was so pendiente and would talk to you. She would massage you and kindly wipe your face. I wrote a poem as an ode to the nurse who took care of you. It will be in our book. I remember when she found out that you had died. The nurse was so sad, she had to leave the room. You always had that affect one people. Everyone loved and still loves you. During the reading I had with Baca and Carlos Carrasco, I thanked him for being so kind to you. I know you liked him, he was the best and so amazing with me during our reading. You would've loved it.

There is so much more that we will talk about. It helps to share all this with you. All these emotions that I've been carrying within my depression and anxiety. Thank You for being there.

I Miss You!

Adrian Ernesto Cepeda

I Wasn't Always the Devoted Son
*"Scars have the strange power to remind us
that our past is real."*
– Cormac McCarthy

>It always started the instant I would
arrive from the West Coast, the distance
would be our buffer, but when I you
saw me, Mami, you would always
start off with a whisper, por qué
no vives in Tejas? Already asking
why I live in la ciudad de Los Angeles,
trying not to let my wife overhear
your tone, when you know the reasons
I live far from home. It is the incident
we never speak of, the secret that night
in the old house when I was watching
futbol with my older hermano and
you came up to see what we were
up to, I was clutching my drink
and without thinking, I asked,
por favor can you get me some
more? The look in your sight
was one of fury when you grabbed
my copa de vidrio and smashed it
on my knee, I still remember
the shattering in the dark, shadows
of glass from the TV, looking down
seeing the mark you created sangre
so bloody. I never let you regret,
forget, how could I? Now looking
back, the pieces so many we could
never find still left on the carpet,
kept our familia apart, we never
mentioned el incidente, the distance

made the gash smart— although,
I don't recall you ever apologizing,
I just remember so much la tensión
between the silence, we never spoke
of your moment of intensity, instead
you would whisper passive aggressively
I was far from the devoted son, loved
speaking back, cursing, su hijo grosero
forgive you, I did, yet, now I already
miss from la lesión you left, now shard
disentangling deeper inside, what did I learn
from this one secreto you scarred into me?

Mami,
I'm Not Ready to See You–
Casi, Not Yet

As I swallow this pill,
I can hear you, back
en mi mente, reminding
me to tómalo con juicio
when it goes down I feel
fighting the virus en mi
garganta, think of all
your battles, hospital
dialysis IV's, too many
surgeries, I remember
them all, although I swallow
this antibiotic, my prescription,
I always follow is to never
forget, te recuerdo
Mami, as this pill goes
down, I believe
you are ayudándome,
battling adentro, eternally.

Dónde Estás

What happened when I saw
you take those last gasps
from the hospital bed,
where have you gone?
I still have so many cosas
things left to ask, I miss
the way you would listen,
hear me, no matter how
near or far, now I wonder
when I look outside at night
time did you fly, te volaste
into the ether, space, clouds
I look are you the estrella
star I see from my window
or are you still soaring farther
away, into other galaxies
passing voyager altísimo
exploring planetas, if I would
look through my telescope
could I feel you near Venus?
Each minute that passes,
I wish I could reach for you
but as I look at your ashes
glowing so brightly above me
I know when I touch these keys
you are always cerca closer
never apart, as your hints
becoming lines and I still
heed every whisper I picture
so near, you loved to impart.

Feeling So Useless
[In the shadow of her drool]

I remember she would sit there
so many RX flowing inside
of her system with some kind
of telenovela blaring in her room
on her favorite chair, it would
feel like she was almost not
there, leaning over crooked
glasses slipping down on
the bridge of her nose, so
pale and white, and this is
mi Mama, who mi Papi
would lovingly call Negrita,
describing her tan Colombiana
cuerpo, but now she's all
flushed as if I can see wings
already forming behind her
merging with the afternoon
light beaming through those
even whiter curtains. I remember
walking slow barefoot on carpet
looking to see if she was still
breathing, my heart underneath
my own skin beating tense,
and me coming up to her and
all I remember was all that drool
hanging from her lips, the same

Speaking con su Sombra

boca that would share advices,
cuentos chistosos and it was always
the same, me walking up to mi Mami
startling her awake, as if she had
arrived, clipping wings from
cielos gate, asking me, "¿tienes
hambre?" If I want something
to eat, when all I wanted
was to take away any doubt
of belief even from the hallway,
that mi Mami truly never
wanted to wake up
and was hoping this time
her wings would take her
to space in the clouds
where pain disappears
and she wouldn't have
to hide all complaints
agony lingers as I watch her
spilling her half empty drink
in the shadow of her drool,
silence returns, as mi Mami
Falls leaning forward, back
feeling so useless, watching
her lie there, hoping she would
arise one last time, and with her
embrace she would magically
taking away the painful face
of her favorite fool.

Adrian Ernesto Cepeda

Will I Ever Be?

I wasn't ready to hear
the silence when she
didn't call, to tell me
she wouldn't be there
for our date, during
high school, no love,
no roadmap for all
this dead-end rejection
that this boy will feel–
no longer this playground
puppy love was no longer

pretend. I wasn't ready
when she dropped me off
at New Years, no more
sparks beyond us, just
explosive looks of fireworks,
above us, just doubt clouds
of remembrance, what
happened to our first
kiss, our first time when
our skins rhymed, as
she drove off I realized
I wouldn't be waking up
next to her nakedly, ever

again. I wasn't ready
when Winnie would
never bark when
unlocking our front
door, or unable to
feel all the times Lucy's
tail could never curl
and Dezi's stinky breath

would never awaken
me sweetly, how I still
miss the infinite scratching
the cuteness that revealed
the paws, the softness

of my furriest friends.
I wasn't ready for her
first surgery, nor
the second one when
they flattened her face,
mi Mami unrecognizable
but she survived that one
her weekly rings still would
nag me. Until the last one,
still not ready to face her
silence. who will answer
my questions, will I ever

be ready, to not ever
face her not calling,
on Tuesday's the finality
of my last words, palabras
unsaid, just the aftertaste
of dead air, so many last
words left unrhymed, all
these voices, always unready
to unhear quietly like the gift
of la música she gave me
still spinning eternally
dawning in my head,
this is the end, spelling out
those same six letters,
one space and the period–
I never ever want to taste
the aftertaste of this sentence
of those words ever again

Adrian Ernesto Cepeda

You are so Right, Kate

Emotionally, it feels like
I've been hit by a car,
Tuesday's are worst,
these are the days I would
speak to mi Mami
on the phone. It feels like
a huge part of my life,
my everlasting light, the one
who has supported my writing,
my poetry, my voice the most
has been extinguished. Excised
there is a gap, so wide, a hole
that is making me feel backspaced,
half-empty, want to somehow
find a way to fill up
this emptiness. It's been two
weeks and I feel like I've aged
so much, so I write, trying
to reignite the memory
of the one who believed
in my rhymes, I still
can't believe that she
is not here, we were planning
on visiting her, time ran out,
the hour glass pours so much
sadness, waves keep on splashing
lost in my tank, today there is no
drive, I feel like my gauge is on E,
wandering today lost in reflection
if I was a ballot you could make me
absentee.

Here Come the Waves

I can feel the splashing
coming from the end,
tears keep on gushing
reliving all the flashing
when we all saw her leave
us, lying in that hotel bed,
gargling of breaths, like
she was slowly drowning
wanting to reach my hand,
but feeling so helpless,
every time the tides return
must deeper and deeper,
crashing inside, wishing
I could hear her speaking
would trade anything
if I could even feel her
resounding all the fury,
now that she has floated
away in silence, I would
love, give anything to hear
mi Mami's voice
addressing me once again.

Mi Mami Always Haunting my Fear

She left in my mind,
remember how she told
me about a lifelong friend
had a ceaseless cold
and one day she died–
even though her words
leaped inside, even now
twenty years later,
that mi Mami's gone,
it's like she can hear me
coughing and some nights
I fear so much closer
to her other side.

All I Feel is Miedo Fear

As la muerte comes for you
oh, so clear, within this
hospital room, mis ojo eyes
already floored, standing
in the puddles of my tears,
reaching for my pulma, verses
calling through each dolor
refrain, although each ink
line wet with lament begins
to smear, I embrace, gripping
this piece as each dripping
rhyme speaks to me–
this grief, I must explore

Adrian Ernesto Cepeda

Sin Ti

*"If we're caught in a wave,
I will carry you over"*
– Martijn Gerard Garritsen

        I was sailing solo
        without a paddle,
        barco, raft or velero
        the current was so hueco
        so much océano vast
        on high tide, nowhere
        to seconder, from
        surges coming desde
        adentro sunburnt mi cuerpo
        all pruned without
        your presence, I looked
        to you my compass,
        holding your crystal
        remains with sunlight
        but now there's just
        sky, glowing through
        your glass radiating
        so many preguntas
        all the answers never
        could subside, sin ti–
        in the middle of this
        tidal, aprendí to swim
        solo, what helped reach
        my island of mine mismo
        forget el machismo,
        wrote letters I finally

unbottled from inside,
I watch them sailing
from each wave reaching
up to el cielo, you taught
me to see hasta mañana
instead goodbye, although
you are a flame cremated
I am no longer afraid to
reach beyond mi miedo
every morning we connect
on this sea, I listen
for your guia, siempre
me llevas with every
wave, on this tide
high, cada mañana, I
greet you hola, no más
shivering, can you feel
me glimmering–
solo sailing, con tu
presencia ola braves this
marinero poético,
not just found mi fuerza
I discovered my own
inner fresca–and now
I am no longer terrified.

Adrian Ernesto Cepeda

Why Do I Keep Picturing...?

…the fire and ashes
engulfing her sweetest
eye lashes, los mismos
we would raise when she
would loudly giggle, when
we would share clásico
Colombian riddles. Her
sonrisa that once adorned
her cheeky cara, glowing
face always showing sunlight
despite all the darkness
slowly devouring her
infierno from the inside,
wishing I could erase all
her angustia, dolor, taking
away her color, all
her remains are now ashes
from the fire, trying not
to picture el lumber, no more
gritos ni llorando, instead
you enciendo los canciones
we shared together, will
spin forever, all that is lit
en mis mente loves to reignite
the sounds of her precioso
refrain.

Las Últimas Palabras

The last words I spoke to her
standing on the doorway
one year ago, during our final
embrace, somehow, I knew
deep inside, that this abrazo
would be la última vez
I would have to thank her
for all the rhymes–I said
Mami, gracias por la poesía
thanking her for the gift
of poetry she shared with
me every palabra trace.
I have learned to savor
every line that appeared
on my lengua tongue
when I recite these stanzas
feeling renacido alive
in my mouth, mi boca,
loving the resounding verso
exhales flavors of each poetic
aftertaste, more than just words
on a page, when I read la poesía
she speaks with me, glowing
luz on my face, they can see
the last line has become my fate
as her presencia is now a verbal
regalo treasure with the latest
rhyme draft, I love to recreate.

Adrian Ernesto Cepeda

Like a Camera Shuttering

When I snap focusing back
on frames, once clear now
hazy distant, looking at this
moment my lens refocuses
those cumpleaños candles
no longer lúcido, flickering
now I see myself sporting
black as if one day I knew
I would be mourning and
you in white, mirroring
your new cloudy color
the spirit free from all
the hospital gowns you
suffered through and you
were just mi Mami and her
and son, posing together
in a family photo. Did I
realize once the camera
snapped, how could I ever
know? You would be taken
ruminating, so many years later,
on my favorite Polaroid memory
so much I am missing, as I keep
reflecting, I can hear the camera
shuttering future asked questions,

Speaking con su Sombra

always flashing for an-
swers...
I keep missing, how much
I want to leap back in live
focus on that moment
now, still in my arms
clutching this image
so much space, you seem
so distant, fragile behind
the glass, reflecting
all that remains–
this after dinner photo
framing the last supper
filling up our final embrace.

All She Said

Most times in the afternoon,
en la mañana or in the darkness
shadow at midnight, I can hear
her voz, like a radio connection
speaking so clearly resounding
inside me, recalling all her advice,
advisos, like *Los Malos son Para
Los Bienes,* Mi Mami always knew
the perfecto saying to make
those overcast clouds disappear
with her palabras de luz she loved
to light her consejos over el teléfono,
more than her calling, *piénsalo bien,
muchacho*, she always knew what
lightbulb advises her hijo needed
to ear—while I miss the sounds of her
daily guidance as her dial time now
remains too silent, now, more than ever
before, her words ring clear sparking
sonrisa son beams pricelessly drying
all my tears with the most sonriente
dichos like *hablando del Rey de Roma,*
those *asoma* words flash to return
all she said like tranquilo magic–
reconnects, her memory voice
always knows when to reappear.

Sabes Lo Que Pienso

Cuando canto las páginas
de poemas en mi corazón;
of all the storied words
your son could tell–
me encantan tus palabras
y recuerdo tus consejos
like memories engraved
like home; lo reflejo
todo, when I write
alone, siempre lo pienso
because your voice
has always shown–
después de todos estos
años, los consejos
de Rosa–tenían toda
la razón.

Detrás de la Ventana Mirando Afuera

Before sueños would arrive,
I remember the film noir-ish
outline making shadow
reflexiones over her face,
as she glared afuera, outside,
her dedos inside her nariz.
When I saw her there, more
than just nose picking, I knew
it was safe to close mis ojos,
when she stood there, staring
down the boogie men, diablo
ghosts, el cucuy of la noche,
this was the only time I felt
safe to dormir, watching
mi Mami digging out her
mocos at bedtime, no need
to count oveja sheep overhead
when she was protecting us
standing like a warrioress at
la ventana, I knew our dreams
were ready to drift off into sleep.

¿Qué Recuerdo, y me Hace Más Falta?

La risa always rising lighting
her voz. No matter la distancia
Mi Mami was always there
to share a chiste, los cuentos
mas lindos or her long distance
giggle. Most all I miss the way
she listened, and loved share
the gift of songs, all the jazz,
the azul in her classical choices,
she glowed ritmos, contagious
vida, her belief in me was something
I learned to believe in. All these palabras,
words, all my verses, every poema
is all because of her. She believed
in me when I didn't have the strength
and courage to believe in myself.
When I speak, she is always
with me, when I laugh, I feel
her still inside, some moments
I need to remind myself, remember
that Mami has left us, because she
is always inside, me, you, in all
of us, more than a memoria,
the energy she shared, is here,
like her spirit that grows every day
everywhere for all us to embrace,
I will miss harnessing all the knowledge
and consejo advice she loved to bestow.
I know some of you will ask…¿Qué
recuerdo, y me hace más falta? Most
of all I miss never having to glimpse
the brilliante glow of mi Mami's most
illuminating face.

Adrian Ernesto Cepeda

Mi Mami Talks to her Plantas

With each spray,
her ojos, become
so misty eyed,
in el jardín, her fortress
de soledad, as she waters
mi Mami whispers
to her potted amigas,
sometimes I imagine her
strolling through la peluquería.
In this salon these plants
are her best and only friends
who do not spread chisme
just bloom and florecer
with cheer in this garden
botánica, only she can hear
their lenguas, they all wait
for her voice, echo rising
like la luz her sonrisa
palabras soft surcando
seeds, when they feel
her footsteps coming
they love to lean in
to hear her, in between
los pajaritos cantando,
she can almost feel
their conversations grow.

Past Medianoche

I was on my laptop
fingers creating música
on keys con mi poesía
as you walked into
Papi's home office,
while Michelle slept
in the other room, as
as the LED luz glowed
from mi computadora,
I could tell from your
sonrojo cheeks, seeing
you brillante smiling,
on the first night we
landed in San Antonio,
already asking me, You're
going to marry her?
Even you knew from
the primer día I introduced
Michelle to you that she
was more than mi novia–
la señora soñando in my old
cuarto, mi musa amor for el
poema de nuestra vida, even
your exaltados eyes already
envisioning our futuro
matrimonio, as the wall clock
chimed past medianoche, you
could instantly picture from
my own ojos, Michelle
becoming my future wife.

Adrian Ernesto Cepeda

La Nochebuena
Mil Novecientos Ochenta y Cinco

I remember unable to dormir
Christmas Eve 1985, seeing
the light in the bedroom,
Mami y Papi on la cama
mirando each other con
ropa puesta and from
the hallway, more than
just hablando, I overhead
my parents conversing,
riendo, as I crept on
la alfombra, seeing the
way they gazed lovingly
with their ojos on each
other, glowing the kind
of amor, I will always
recuerdo, when I ponder
the definition of a feliz
matrimonio I blink back
to my parents on the bed
toda la noche using their
labios y bocas to convesar
cariñosamente—I will nunca
olvidaré the giggling resounding
loudly in their bedroom
mi Mami y Papi tingling
closer with their clothes on
en la Nochebuena, their voices
cantando en mi memoria
a tradition on their aniversario
with the lights on, every year,
enthralled by their own

palabras after thirty years,
while other couples would
drift further away from one
another while snoring asleep,
en our casa mi Mami y Papi
would reawaken melting
renewed stories like
newlyweds, cada año
así es como mis padres
loved to reconnect.

What do I remember?

Mi Mami was always there
to share a chiste, cuento or
long distance giggle. Most
all I miss the way she listened,
and loved share the gift of songs,
all the jazz, the azul in her classical
choices, she glowed ritmos, contagious
vida, her belief in me was something
I learned to believe in. All these palabras,
words, all my verses, every poema is all
because of her. She believed in me
when I didn't have the strength
and courage to believe in myself.
When I speak, she is always
with me, when I laugh, I feel
her still inside, some moments
I need to remind myself, remember
that Mami has left us, because she
is always inside, me, you, in all
of us, more than a memoria,
the energy she shared, is here,
like her spirit that grows every day
everywhere for all us to embrace.

Everything I Write

With every line
break, stanza, poem
I ever begun,
every rhyme you
feel, hear and see,
today with all
my emotions
ringing clear, reminding
you from me, her son–
these verses I recite
now becoming rays
reflecting this, I can selflessly
say, of all the mothers
we know, who glowed–
to me, our Mami will
always remain–
the greatest one.

Adrian Ernesto Cepeda

The Son Who Brings You Sonrisas

Our light-hearted banter rings long
distanced. I love bringing los chistes
to uncork your laughter unbottled like
precious champagne–

toasting more sunrises & feel your
glasses over-flowing… We need you to
keep drinking Buenos Días, forever after
wishes, sometimes sipping

half full; no more hang ups, I always
listen–I remember Yesterday once was
your favorite refrain. I know the pain
keeps calling these

thorns may keep stinging, we love your
voice especially when your singing…
cantas estas promesas y las palabras, I
always send, para mi

Mami: necesitamos respirar para seguir
creyendo;
para Mañana su sonrisa está llamando–
your son will rise again.

As I stand by Her Mar

Even the sand below
me know, this is not
goodbye, how could
I ever say adiós when
I feel you closer like
whispers from el viento
when I write I can hear
the heir of you, beautifully
shadowing me with gusts
that shine when I recite
this poem, even the breeze
knows your son is no longer
alone, when my fingers
hit the keys we converse
in palabras, your consejos
reflecting back like waves
from the ocean, even when
I drift off sailing in daydreams
I picture you sunglasses
next to me, with every line
you Mami answer me back
in a voice that reaches
out, coming clearer
although I miss your
glow, every poem I write–
loves resonating you.

What Does She See?

When I look inside
my Mama's terrified
eyes, blinking like she
wants to speak at me,
the only sounds I hear
is her breathing saliva
heavy, eyelids flashing
some kind of code Morse
I wish I could decipher.
Seeing this once Phoenix
no longer rising like
a Lazarus señora lady
once invincible, now
she in this hospital bed
the one who would
overshadow me, protect
and advise is now a shadow
of her once fierce self.
Seeing her eyes, so close
and yet so far away–

I am all ears, Mama…

Speaking con su Sombra

I want to feel what she
is trying to tell me. Although
her ojos are the windows all
that comes out... Her once
voice of fire, whose luz
has now turned out cold.
Bo sounds just the slow
—blinking, silence, tears
of her corazón, slowing
down once enlightening
no longer fighter, I fear
not ever hearing Mama's
laughter glowing, no more
I keep waiting for her
arise, reawaken and call
me but she's still–
with no answers.

Adrian Ernesto Cepeda

I Always Remember Dialing

A payphone–
those ancient now extinct relics found
on almost every calle street corner, some
had booths but usually they hung
on walls outside of supermarkets,
drugstores and malls, before cells
and smart Apple phones, we would
take our loose change and call our friends,
lovers and familia members. And sometimes

with no quarters–
I would try calling mi Mami, I recall
her number would ring, she would
answer saying *A-lo!* While trying
to speak into the receiver nothing
came out, my voice was blocked–
with no quarters you could dial
someone but they could never
hear you. When I want to talk to her

this is what it feels like–
1987 and I am redialing her phone
number. She picks up and says
mi nombre as I try to speak,
yelling, Mami, it's me su hijo
but she can never hear me. This
is when I wake up with a sore

throat always hoping maybe
I can go back–
but then I realize
there is no payphone.
I sit up breathing panicky,
grasping the nightmare, mi Mami
still dead. There was no call,
I just keep replaying her voice
hearing mi Mami, recalling–
I can never again answer
her ringing inside my head.

Adrian Ernesto Cepeda

Poesía Incompleta

What do I do with all
the love I have for her?
Where do I put it? Who
share this cariño with?
I used to drink it, try
swallowing it all away
at the bottom of a shot
glass, but now I want
to keep it uncorked
savor the aromas I kept
bottled down for so long–
I want to toast her, for
the peace she gave me
and all the ones that got
in the way. I keep thinking
of her last palabras, how
she sounded in the shadows
of the front door before
saying her despedidas
for la última vez, if I knew
it was the last time, I would
have filmed it with every cell
of my iPhone, recorded her
voz, left every one of her
voice mensajes saved. Now
what will I do for all the love
I am saving for her, pensando
of all the words I will ever
oir again, just for a moment,
I would trade every single
one of my possesions prized,
first edition Bell Jar libro,
mono Beatles For Sale, disco
Imagine unboxed, just to hear
her closely every palabra, consejo,
I never wanted to hear, now
I wish I would have...

El Milagro of Light

Some nights, I can
still see, remembering her
fear blinking loudly gasping
the most silent llorando
of cries, her last moments
engraved, eternally mi Mami
still haunts me, glaring
back at me en la noche
when the lamp and flickering
lightbulbs are off, her ojos
still mirándome, every night
in my mind, I feel her
breaths tremble, trying
to respirar, I can hear
her slowly struggling
for palabras, inside–the fear

she could never share, always
stares back, but at least I was
there next to her, el hijo, the sun,
by her side, seeing her softly
soar off silently, I picture
replaying this last scene, I miss
her most at night, en mi mente,
remember the agridulce miracle
watching how radiantly bright
our Mami was when she left
us, her ojos distantes signaling
to me no more miedo to hide...
witnessing el último momento
as her soul rose–
merging beautifully
into el milagro of light.

Adrian Ernesto Cepeda

Nunca te Dije

Mami. I am sorry for all our disputa arguments
heated when I cursed, swore, fuck, shit, like
gasoline poured over my palabras just to see
you blush Rosa furiosa mis malas palabras
more than furiously inflamed you

Lo lamento for every mentira, I ever sold you,
I could never tell you about all the shots, lines
I snorted, tabs I swallowed, trips, rolls or the night
I accidentally swallowed ten hits of acid during
Mardi Gras. I was trying to numb mi dolor of pain.

I am sorry for the times I ended up borracho
drunk, passed out en la carpeta, falling after
another round of 'off to the races' you loved
to call it, oyendo hearing me racing
from mi cuarto to el baño.

Lo lamento for all the tiempo
I was ashamed of our last nombre,
our lengua, our familia, I was always
the spoiled niño, who not only slayed
his Mami with words but once even
made his own Papi llorar.

I am sorry I never told you, Mami,
I was your mad gringo,
I loathed the idea of mi myself,
For so many años, I couldn't
Even stand seeing this flaco
face en el espejo mirror.

Lo lamento of my own inner
Odio hate, I was disgusted

Speaking con su Sombra

And I ran to find some ganas
some bolas, some fuerza
in every cuidad I sought
to become a true Cepeda
but I kept corriendo
running from you.

I am sorry for hiding
the miedo child I never
wanted to be. I was failing
by hiding and not trying
it was mi falta, it wasn't
until I started escribir
mis poems that my voz
rediscovered my fuerza
purpose para mi vida.

Lo lamento for forgetting
your cumpleaños, to not
llamar you still haunts me
cada día, how could I even
forget, olividar? I am sorry

for el dolor and pain, I caused
you, when I couldn't help you
with my broken body cuerpo
parts, I was damaged so much–

tomado y adicto pero no
necesitaba eso, I only need
mi esposa, mi familia, tú–
I am sorry for all the times
I forgot to say gracias,
All of this is because of you.

Adrian Ernesto Cepeda

¿A Dónde Vas?

She asked watching me
float farther away through
the Great Lakes as I crossed
rivers in Mississippi... Río
Grande, passing through oceans
Atlantic, in France it was all
about the Seine even the Salton
could see... I would drift further
inside every time with every wave
hoping with each low and high
tide, I could finally find the current
flow of my own río. Although
I would sail alone, I felt her stirring
aviso's as I rowed, I always paddled
deeper rippling to create surges
of poems skin pruned, frío waves
her treasured reminders always
carry me sailing towards
home. When I was embarking
there were momentos in times
I felt like sinking astray,
I would ask myself, what if
I strayed? But then evening
noches would carry me
my skin luna eclipsed this

deep end despite my fears,
within splashes and lágrimas,
que lloro all my tears, would
you believe, I embraced
every guidance gift, a regalo
I unwrapped your map
in the present, mi estrella
direction– always oyendo
Mami's voz– sigue
moviendo hijo through each
transiting connections, en este
viaje, and through all these
journeys, remember–
I always waded for you.

Adrian Ernesto Cepeda

Orlando to Key West
[FLA road trip circa 1980]

I remember the white Chevy
Rent-a-car that would rumble
to a stop like an old viejo
waking up from a long deep
afternoon nap, the car would
stop shaking a few seconds
after mi Papi would take
the key out of the ignition.
I recall all the rest stops,
200 miles from Mickey
At Walt Disney World
down the Florida Turnpike
and Hemingway's house
with all the gaticos, mi Mami
although allergic to their fur
definitely wanted to see...
with our own ojos, I remember
midnight gas station fill ups
the car having even longer
seizures before stopping,
early AM diners with laminated
flavors of eggs, bacon, ham,
pancakes, toast– you could
almost eat off the glossy
menus. I can almost taste
the little packets of jelly
at the side of our booth
grape always my favorite.
I recall our FM radio theme
song "Feliz Navidad"
Jose Feliciano's static
voice playing over and over
during our familia December
vacations. Mi Papi drove us
so long until we stopped right

before Key West, as we pulled
over the car convulsing
to an even more trembling
stop at the side of the road,
shimmering water glowing
in between us, as we slept
in our seats, napping
in the car, the southern
most sun above us, barely
keep my eyes open glaring
at the waves, remember
that the Mobile attendant
while pumping our gas
claiming we could see Cuba
from the highway. All
I remember was blinking
imagine picturing Fidel's
cigar smoke rising above
the ocean but all I saw
bursting clouds, relaxing
sea waves, salt-water air
sweating from the windows
rolled down, I just wanted
to swim in my daydreams,
but deep sleep splashed me
even mi Papi's front seat
snoring couldn't keep me
awake as the soaring seagulls
serenaded us like sheep,
thirty years later, I can
almost hear their peaceful
squawking, with the sleepy sol in
my sight–
carsick smiles inside
my head,

                    I still envision...
                    and I am back
                    there drifting off
                    unbuckling daydreams
                    in the middle seat...

I Saw You in Mis Sueños, Last Night

We were in this casa
and I was in this room,
glaring at the closet. And
you Mami were sitting there
patiently like you used to,
with your purse on your
knees, quietly dressed up
and then we were walking
in an airport. So many people
it was the largest aeropuerto
I have ever seen, but nobody
was holding any luggage,
bags or maletas. The travelers
were all going through these
revolving doors outside into
the light, it's as if this terminal
was the last stop before heaven.
I recall before you walked
through las puertas giratorias
I saw you looking very hungry
and I asked, *¿Tienes hambre?*
¿quieres comer antes de su
vuelo? I will never forget
before you walked solo into
la luz, just like a poet you
looked at me and replied

in inglés, I want to eat Jazz.
There was no music, after
you left, for a moment,
I was stuck in doors
as if it was not time for
me to leave, so this
muy amable hombre,
who was coming through
the other side, helped back
into the dusky indoor part
of the airport. I had shorts
on and was wearing a vintage
1980s Members Only
chaqueta unzipped. I recall
just roaming around seeing
everyone feliz joyously
in a Las Vegas mood with
dim casino lights and candles
barely lighting up these rooms
and I kept wandering around
alone, feeling cold looking
for more light.

Adrian Ernesto Cepeda

¿Cuándo Dejaste de Hablar con Dios?

I remember los Domingos
in the morning you would
vestirse in a flowering Sunday
dress, all white with splashes
of a colorful pintura, ready
to heed las palabras de God–
I remember the light cheeks
rosa red, glowing on your face,
when you returned from
la Iglesia treasuring all
the words after speaking
con Dios and un día–
you stopped all went silent
with your savior. The dress
gathered holy dust inside
your closet and you rarely
ever spoke of el buen libro.
¿Por qué? Why did you stop
listening to Dios? Was it
after your Mother or our
abuelita murió? Después
tu Papa our abuelito Jose
followed your Mama
to el Cielo? Was it after
your first surgery when
you lost sight in one of
your ojos? Did you not
want to oir what God
wanted to explicar and
tell you the reasons? I
always wondered que
paso to your Domingo
dress? I imagine the
flowers once blooming
now wilting en la oscuridad–
waiting for you to slip
on and feel Sunday again,
but you did feel the holy
fabric and not want to
hear the explanations

Speaking con su Sombra

from above. So, you turned
up la música clásica, instead,
playing the loudest violins
so Dios can hear them en
la noche instead of prayers
you would beautifully
turn up the strings to cover
up the voz of Dios in heaven.
There were no reasons for
all the dolor, you could no
longer heed the words nor
escuchar what Dios was
mouthing to you. Even so,
I nunca heard you reconociste
or ever acknowledged
the lords nombre even
in your worst angustia pain.
Are you now speaking, now
no longer estranged? imagining
the conversations once so
close, are you still keeping
your distancia to Dios? In
the after vida, I picture
you wearing the Domingo
dress, as the flowers flow
trying to convince to you
to listen to las plantas,
after all these años
so many exhausted palabras
are ready to be arisen,
this blessed communication
of all you kept inside can
devoutly be addressed, even
now, beyond contemplative
reflection, when you are ready
to overhear each ruminative
confession floating from
hymn emanating quietly still
inside your own privado space.

Adrian Ernesto Cepeda

The Movie House is Our Church
"And I believe there's a spirituality in films, it's as if movies answer an ancient quest for the common unconscious. they fulfill a spiritual need that people have to share a common memory."
– Martin Scorsese

> When she stopped speaking
> to Dios, Mami would take us
> to our new Iglesia, where todos
> loved descubriendo faith in films,
> in our familia, celluloid was
> celestial. En la oscuridad,
> so many lessons, we learned
> to stop fearing Cucuy, Predator
> Aliens, melting Nazi faces,
> snakes in Temple of Doom
> in the dark, we longed for
> Peter Venkman's fearlessness
> as he hilariously stood, mis
> hermanos and I sat cantando
> we no longer "afraid of no
> ghosts." We looked forward
> to experiencing divinity
> in the dark, discovering
> the Force, instead of raising
> fits with my brothers, we
> wanted to be like Crusaders
> in Capes, fighting el crimen,
> soaring arriba en el cielo
> leaping tall buildings,
> y nunca olvidando el beso
> de forgetfulness between

Clark Kent and Lois Lane.
We todos were all cautivados
by the motions, pictures
when the lights dimmed
reading palabras that scroll
on the Star Wars screen.
Looking up at the front,
seeing la luz of the projector
witnessing Maltese Falcons
Casa's Blanca, Streetcars
named deso, La Dolce Vita,
reigniting new visions all in
black and white, when
Mami no longer practiced
her prayers, las películas
became our cinematic
gospels. With our ojos
abiertos, experiencing estrellas
of delight from our estadio
chairs, mi Mami invited us
every Sunday to this palace
de adoración where we all
believed the movie house
was our church, todos
creyendo in sacred screen's
big, seeing spirits holy enlarged.

En este Oscuro día de Noviembre 2017

When the light rose, from
the afternoon neblina,
glowing inside your intensive
car hospital room, leading
you up before our ojos
we could see your eyes
drift away beautiful sadness
filled the room, we could
feel el dolor evaporate,
as el sol came out shimmering
brillante por ti, I remember
sitting there before witnessing
your final exhales, wanting
to hear your voz before
the paleness took over
your rosa cheeks, the tears
pouring like rain, shower
forecast even more lágrimas

Speaking con su Sombra

today, even now, recordando
este día Noviembre 2017,
tres años después as I write
this, because I was there,
flew in ojos rojos nocturno
flight, to see you soaring
into that noche buena night,
your presencia appears
in all our vidas, every
morning te escribe, when
mi Papi y mis hermanos
hablarte, speaking to your
crystal, cuando vemos
the crystal glowing
we can hear you proudly
brillando sunlight sonrisas
feeling closer every mañana
as you reawaken, when las
cortinas se abren, we experience
you as this gift reopening
through la preciosa presence
of your beaming luz.

Adrian Ernesto Cepeda

Driving Us Back to the Hospital [in Joe's Car]

When my brother died my sister and I wept. I don't know what happened, one of us triggered laughter in the other. But it's all right, we knew the depth of our sorrow, so it was alright ... because that's what life is—it's "the fearful symmetry" of Blake, you know, joy and sorrow. You don't just want to feel one of them. They are both valuable to the spirit.

> – Patti Smith
> We knew Mami was waiting
> for us with her final blinks
> before drifting off in her ICU
> bed. All three of us hermanos,
> full of silencio, our ojos all
> cried out of tears, as Joe
> signaled to exit past 281
> before 1604, at the stop sign,
> three brothers turned to each
> other, before she died, and
> we laughed, howling together
> just like we used to in those
> Burlington street days, before
> Georgetown Ave., move to
> Laredo, Papi separating from
> Mami as he packed his bags
> to San Antonio, now inside
> this car, in la cuidad del Alamo,
> on the way back to her hospital
> room, for a moment we had
> dived inside exhausted risitas,
> just for a second to free the sorrow
> that surrounded us, caught in
> the car with cathartic giggles

before the llorando returns,
I could hear Mami's voice
en el carro asking us: ¿Están
echando cuentos, solos? Qué
chistosos! I know she could
feel the nervousness of our
exalted laughter, blushing
puffy sad cheeks rojos eyes
as our little hermanito Joe
manejando despacio towards
the top of the hill, on our way
to see Mami alive for la
última vez, no cuentos,
just miedo for the loss that
would wash over, tidal us–
as mourning's sombra waiting
to shower us with a lifetime
of angustia– no amount
of laughing could stop
the sadness soaking
my brothers and I, nosotros
crecimos as rivales but on
that day, we were rivals
peliando no más– fighting
it no more, already drowning
in duelos torrential refrain,
all three of us no longer
afraid in Joe's car together
unidos closer en tristeza's
embrace.

"Is it foolish to speak of little joys that occur in the middle of tragedy? It is our humanity. Whatever we have left of it. We must not deny it to ourselves."
– Ilya Kaminsky

Adrian Ernesto Cepeda

Afterword

One of my poet heroes, Patti Smith, once described the passing of the late great Allen Ginsberg as being a 'nice death.' When mi Mami transitioned from this earth, there was nothing nice about her death. The moment when she died was beautiful and poetically moving, and is a memory that will be engraved in my mind por siempre, but when she died it was anything but nice.

This collection of poems came to life after mi Mami died. Mi Papi handed me a large sealed yellow and gold envelope of poems that held all of the poemas I had written for mi Mami for the past ten years. For months afterwards, even though I was the one who had crafted these verses for her, I could not bring myself to open the envelope. It was so difficult for me. The words inside were the poems she held, treasured, and saved. I just couldn't bring myself to open and reread all the words I had written for her.

I finally opened the envelope of my poems after her memorial service. There was something that Maria Emma, a lifelong friend of our familia, said to me before the service and that is she loved my poetry, especially the way I had blended English and Spanish within the poems. Her words had left an impression on me and when I went through all the poems, I realized that I needed to compile all of them, plus all the new poemas that she had inspired before and after she died. My goal was to craft a collection of poemas in mi Mami's honor.

This collection is a living ode to mi Mami who always was my number one supporter and believed in me and my talents, as she saw the promising gift in my words before I answered the calling as a poeta. I know I would not be a published poet if it wasn't for the encouragement and belief from mi Mami. It took me years to finish this collection because I avoided facing all the emotions I had buried inside about how I felt about her death. I know there was a tsunami of pain and sadness tidaling inside as there was an incident after watching the 2019 U.S. Open Final where mi Mami's favorite player Rafael Nadal had won the championship after a four-hour classic. As soon as Rafa Nadal won, I broke down in tears and I couldn't stop crying. At that moment, I realized mi Mami was dead and I couldn't call her on the telephone and celebrate this win. This realization caused my tsunami of emotions to burst. I hadn't cried that hard since she first died. Still, just like the envelope of poems that I couldn't open, I needed more time to complete this collection.

I found myself fearful of finishing this book, and because of the emotional outburst that occurred after watching Nadal win, I was not ready to face even more pain and hurt from her passing. For years, I had this fear of death and mi Mami's transitioning had made this fear a reality. During the pandemic, I was inspired by Night Worms, a literary subscription service that sends their members novels and poetry collections with horror themes.
After selecting my fourth book La Belle Ajar, for their readers, I wanted to craft a book of poems that Night Worms and their subscribers would enjoy reading. Mostly, I wanted to face my fear of death so during the Pandemic, the summer of 2020, I crafted We Are the Ones Possessed. Because I had opened up to the idea of death without actually facing my fears, I had a physical, emotional and mental health breakdown soon after completing this manuscript.

After asking and receiving help from my doctor and my therapist, one of the ways that started the healing process was writing these daily letters to mi Mami. I was deeply missing our weekly phone calls, where I could call her and she could lift my spirits and calm any doubts, fears, or anxieties with a sonrisa laugh, a word or advice with her voz of love.

I still write and enjoy writing mi Mami every day. Because of our epistolary connection, we have made this book together. I couldn't have done this without her. This collection would not have been published without mi Mami's help, guidance, and daily assistance. Although she has died, I still can feel her presencia in mi vida and especially in all these poemas. Gracias, Mami por la inspiración. I Miss You! We did it. Our poetry book lives in your honor. Thank you for giving me the gift of la poesia. Now we can share this present with the rest of the world.

Viva La Poesia!
Adrian Ernesto y Rosalba Cepeda

Gracias y Agradecido

Thank You for the support, belief y puro amor to mi esposa Michelle, mi Papi, Rene & Maria, Joe & Chante, Woody Gold, and all the Cepeda's, Bernal's, Busher's, Ferguson's and Cannatelli's around el mundo.

My gratitude to Los Casas: Efraim, Juan and a special gracias to Maria Emma, who was first to realize and encourage me to write in my distinctive bilingual form in which led to Speaking con su Sombra as you are reading today.

Abrazos and Gracias to Alma Luz Villanueva, Jimmy Santiago Baca, Francesca Lia Block, Gayle Brandeis, and Amy Shimshon-Santo for humbling me with your maravilloso blurbs. Thank You also to Carol Rodriguez, Jean-Pierre Rueda, Carlos Mendoza, Leanne Hunt, Andrea Auten and Alisha Grace for reading early drafts and giving your essential feedback on Sombra.

Thank You to all the editors who believed in these poemas and published poems from Sombra: Gayle Brandeis, Lisa Marie Basile, Laura Villareal, Monica Lewis, Rachael De Moravia, Natasha Lioe, Samantha Lamph, Kevin D. Woodall, Emery Ross, Benjamin Selesnick, Rosalyn Spencer and Lenny DellaRocca.

Mil Gracias to Davina A. Ferreira and Alegría Publishing for creer in this very personal passion project and publishing, Speaking con su Sombra this collection of poemas written for, inspired by and dedicated to mi Mami. You honored la lengua in these poems and believing in Sombra when no one else did. I am proud to be published with Alegría. ¡Viva La Poesía!

¡Mami, Lo hicimos! El libro that tú inspiraste has been published by Alegría and not only could I not have done this without you, because we did this los juntos, together, our colección de poemas, Speaking con su Sombra, is out for every one in the world to read. I miss you y gracias por la poesía.

Acknowledgments

Some poems in this book first appeared in the following publications, sometimes in different form:

Alebrijes Review: "I Always Remember Dialing," "I Saw You in Mis Sueños, Last Night"

Breadcrumbs #543: "I Wasn't Always the Devoted Son"

Burning House Press: "¿A Dónde Vas?"

Capsule Stories: "I Wouldn't Want to Take a Pill," "Mi Mami's Nurse Lucilla Practices Tonglen"

Letters From Here to Here After: International Anthology: "Dear Mami"

Luna Luna Magazine: "¿Dónde pongo mi tristeza?", "Sin Ti"

Memoir Mix Tapes: B-Sides: "If Not For You"

Rigorous: "Papi says, I Could Lose 15-20 lbs."

South Florida Poetry Journal: "Thrift Store Mysteries."

Tiferet Journal: "This House Sans Her Spirit"

West Branch: "Mi Mami Talks to her Plantas"

About the autor

Adrian Ernesto Cepeda is the author of So Many Flowers, So Little Time from Red Mare Press, Flashes & Verses... Becoming Attractions from Unsolicited Press, Between the Spine from Picture Show Press and La Belle Ajar & We Are the Ones Possessed from CLASH Books.

His poetry has been featured in Harvard Palabritas, Alebrijes Review, Glass Poetry: Poets Resist, Cultural Weekly, Yes, Poetry, Frontier Poetry, The Fem, poeticdiversity, Rigorous, Luna Luna Magazine, Olney Magazine, The Wild Word, The Revolution Relaunch and Palette Poetry.

Adrian lives with his wife and their adorably spoiled cat Woody Gold in Los Angeles.

You can connect with the poet at: www.AdrianErnestoCepeda.com

www.ingramcontent.com/pod-product-compliance
Lightning Source LLC
Chambersburg PA
CBHW072203100526
44589CB00015B/2339